TABLE OF CONTENTS

The UK Slow Cooker Recipe Book For Beginners and Pros

Quick and Super-Delicious Recipes for Family and Friends

Sarah A. Lewis

WHAT IS A SLOW COOKER?

Slow cookers are plug-in electronic kitchen appliances that use gentle heat to warm up batches of food to a simmer for several hours. They can also be called crockpots. Usually, this common cooking device is used to create dishes that are liquid-based, which allows for a slow and steady heating process.

Often, people leave their slow cookers to cook their meals for the whole day whilst they're away at work. This is partly why they are so popular nowadays, but we will discuss the various benefits of the slow cooker later in the book!

History of the Slow Cooker

Slow cookers first gained popularity back in the 1940s. During this time, women began to work away from home more and more. Because of this, they no longer had time to spend all day in the kitchen cooking dinner for the family.

To overcome this reduction in spare time, women turned to the slow cooker. They could prepare dinner in the morning, pop it into the slow cooker, and leave it to simmer for the whole day whilst they were away at work. When they returned home, they had enough time to finish preparing the food just in time for everybody to sit and enjoy the evening meal together.

It wasn't until the 1970s that large-scale production of slow cookers would begin. With this, they became even more popular. In 1974, slow cookers with removable inserts were first introduced, which made the appliances much easier to clean.

Fast forward to today and slow cookers are much more advanced. Many of them have multiple pre-programmed settings and high-tech heating systems that make slow cooking even simpler and more efficient than ever.

What Are Slow Cookers Made Of?

Usually, slow cookers are made of metal or ceramic because both of these materials are great at conducting and retaining heat. They can also be made using porcelain, but this is less common.

Metal slow cookers are composed of aluminium with a non-stick coating, which makes the appliance light and easy to carry. However, they don't hold their heat as well as other options.

The appliance contains a large, empty vessel where your food is placed, and this sits above a metal heating unit. When this unit receives an electrical current, it starts to heat up. In turn, the food sitting just above it will also heat up.

Every slow cooker comes with a lid that protects your food as it cooks for several hours and prevents any moisture or steam from escaping the pot, as this can slow down the cooking process. The lid also provides protection against splashes and spills as the mixture boils and bubbles.

What Can You Make in a Slow Cooker?

As mentioned above, you can produce a range of dishes that are predominantly liquid based using a slow cooker. Most commonly, it is soups, stews, and casseroles that are created, but you can make pretty much anything.

Whether you love a hearty stew that is packed full of protein and vegetables or a delicious soup that is full of your favourite flavours, you can create the dishes of your dreams using your slow cooker.

Popular ingredients to use in a slow cooker include meats (such as beef, pork, chicken, turkey, and sausages), potatoes, and root vegetables. If you're not a meat-eater, don't worry! There are plenty of meat alternatives that can be used in your slow cooker recipes. In fact, this book includes plenty of vegetarian and vegan recipes for you to try out. You will love these meat-free recipes, regardless of if you usually eat meat or not.

You can fry up your ingredients prior to adding them into the slow cooker if you want to add a bit of extra crisp and crunch, or you can completely skip the frying pan and add your ingredients straight into the device for a softer, mushier texture.

Better yet, cooking with this type of kitchen appliance is super simple and quick. You don't have to be the best cook in the world to enjoy creating tasty recipes in a slow cooker!

It's not just main dishes you can make in a slow cooker. You also have the ability to create delicious breakfasts, lunches, starters, sides, and desserts. You could literally cook a five-course meal in this nifty kitchen appliance!

WHAT IS A SLOW COOKER?

WHERE CAN YOU GET A SLOW COOKER?

Nowadays, there are hundreds of different slow cooker models available for you to buy. In fact, it can get quite overwhelming trying to decide which one will suit you the best!

Depending on your needs and preferences, you might benefit from a particular type of slow cooker. For example, if you prefer to have pre-programmed cooking settings, you will have to choose a model that provides these specific settings. However, most standard slow cookers will operate in a similar fashion, so if you just need a basic cooker, you can go for pretty much any of the options listed below.

Here are some of the best brands that offer high-quality slow cookers for your kitchen.

- Morphy Richards
- Tefal
- Russell Hobbs
- Cookworks
- Lakeland
- Argos
- Amazon
- Curry's

Luckily, every one of these brands is available online so you can easily find the perfect slow cooker for your kitchen, and have it delivered to your door in no time.

HOW DO YOU USE A SLOW COOKER?

HOW DO YOU USE A SLOW COOKER?

Slow cookers are super simple to use. Pretty much anybody, from beginner to professional, can use them to create delicious meals. All you need to do is plug in your slow cooker, add your desired ingredients, give it all a stir, add the lid, and leave it to simmer away for several hours.

The only preparation you need to do is the pre-cooking and chopping of your ingredients. Once they are in the slow cooker, you can leave it for hours without intervention.

When your food is cooked and heated through, all you need to do is turn off the slow cooker or leave it on a 'warm' setting to keep your food hot until you serve it.

Every slow cooker will come with a user manual that is specific to that model. Make sure to give this manual a read before you use your slow cooker for the first time, so you know exactly what each button means!

The manual will also contain details of your warranty. If your machine breaks, you may be eligible to get a replacement, but this will depend on which manufacturer has supplied the slow cooker.

HOW DO YOU USE A SLOW COOKER?

HOW DO YOU MAINTAIN A SLOW COOKER?

HOW DO YOU MAINTAIN A SLOW COOKER?

Slow cookers are much easier to keep clean nowadays. Most of them have removable components that can be easily washed in your kitchen sink or placed in the dishwasher after use.

Top Maintenance Tips for Your Slow Cooker

Here are some of the best maintenance tips to keep your slow cooker looking and functioning as well as it did when you first bought it.

Allow the slow cooker to cool down after you've used it. Once it has cooled to room temperature, remove the inner compartment (the crock) from the heating element. Along with the lid, wash this inner compartment in the sink, and wipe the outside of the slow cooker if there are any spills or splashes. This ensures no dried food gets stuck on the machine.

If there are any dried spots of food that you've missed, they can be tough to get off! To help you remove these, take some baking soda or vinegar and dissolve it in warm water. Apply this to the dry spots and use a bristled brush or a cloth to remove them.

Avoid using harsh scrubbing or very abrasive sponges when cleaning the outer parts of your slow cooker as this could damage the machine.

How to Clean Your Slow Cooker

It's important to clean your slow cooker after every use. This ensures that no tough spots of food dry onto the machine and helps to maintain its function.

Even when your slow cooker looks clean, there might be small spots that you missed the last time you gave it a wipe down. It's a good idea to spend a little bit of extra time cleaning your slow cooker after every few uses to ensure it stays perfectly clean.

Follow these steps to give your slow cooker a much-needed deep clean.

Unplug your slow cooker before cleaning.

Take a clean cloth and dampen it with warm water. Use this to wipe the exterior of the machine. If there are any stubborn spots, add some washing-up liquid to the cloth and give them a good scrub.

Use a toothbrush or a small, bristled brush to get into the small crevices of the machine. You can use this brush to remove any lost crumbs that have fallen under the heating element.

Don't forget to clean the base of the machine too. There could be stains on there!

Remove the interior component from the machine and either wash it with warm water and washing liquid in the sink or add it to your dishwasher on the bottom shelf and put it through a full cycle.

If you don't have a dishwasher, try these steps below as a great alternative.

Fill up your slow cooker with warm water and baking soda until it is around three-quarters full or just above the area where your leftover food line is.

Turn the slow cooker on to low heat, add the lid, and leave it to simmer for an hour.

When the hour is complete, remove the lid and pour out the water

Give the inner parts of the slow cooker a wipe with a clean cloth.

Leave the device out on your kitchen countertop to dry.

BENEFITS OF USING THE SLOW COOKER

The slow cooker provides several benefits, including the ones below.

It's Simple to Use

Slow cookers are suitable for everybody, regardless of your culinary abilities or cooking experience. All you need to do is add your ingredients, turn the cooker on, and leave the machine to do its thing for several hours. Easy!

It's Easy to Clean

Slow cookers can be easily wiped down after use and they are dishwasher friendly. Cooking your meals in a slow cooker also reduces the use of various pots, pans, and utensils, meaning you have less washing up to do after dinner.

It Enables Hands-Off Cooking

You can leave slow cookers for hours without needing to regularly check on them. This means you can focus on other activities and errands while you're waiting for your food to cook, making them perfect if you have a hectic schedule.

It Uses Less Energy

Compared to a standard electric oven or hob, slow cookers use less energy, meaning you can save on the utility bills. Of course, you may still need to use the oven or hob for other meals, but even using the slow cooker a couple of times a week can significantly cut your expenses in the long run.

It Reduces Your Shopping Bill

As slow cookers enable you to prepare your meals in bulk, it reduces unnecessary spending on several ingredients. You can buy similar ingredients to use in multiple slow cooker recipes, meaning you can buy fewer ingredients for the week ahead and you can reduce your food wastage. It also cuts the energy costs associated with preparing your meals separately.

It Promotes Healthy Cooking

If you're not overly keen on your veggies, the slow cooker is a great way to incorporate more of them into your diet. You can easily achieve your 5-a-day by adding multiple portions of vegetables into your meals without compromising on the taste.

Preparing your food with a slow cooker provides a healthier alternative to deep-frying or sauteing. Due to the low temperatures, the chance of overcooking your food is low. The essential micronutrients are retained and the risk of potentially harmful chemicals leaking into your food is reduced.

You Can Make Multiple Portions at Once

If you're looking for a more sustainable way to cook, slow cookers are for you!

Most slow cookers hold large volumes of food, meaning you can prepare multiple portions at once. This saves on time and cost by decreasing the need for multiple ingredients and reducing electricity usage in your home.

Slow cookers are, therefore, perfect for the days where you're cooking for the whole family, having a buffet, hosting a birthday celebration at your house, or you are meal prepping for the week ahead.

It Promotes Variety

There are countless recipes you can create with the slow cooker. From beef stew to chicken casserole to vegetable soup, the list is never-ending. This means you have a huge scope for variety with your slow cooker.

If you're looking for some new and exciting dinners to try, the slow cooker makes this process super easy.

It is Small and Compact

Although most slow cookers can hold large volumes of food, they are usually pretty compact. You can easily keep your device out on the kitchen countertop, neatly tucked away to the side. Alternatively, you can put the slow cooker away in your cupboard to keep your kitchen space clear.

There Are Multiple Varieties

Modern-day technological advancements have brought about a wide variety of different slow cookers. Basic slow cookers usually have low, medium, and high heat settings. You can get more high-tech slow cookers with pre-programmed settings and options that enable you to set a timer on the machine so you can cook your food down to the exact minute.

Now you know the many incredible benefits of using a slow cooker in the kitchen, it's time to try some exciting new recipes!

The following pages will detail several recipes that can be used to make breakfast, lunch, dinner, sides, snacks, and desserts for you and the whole family to enjoy.

BENEFITS OF USING THE SLOW COOKER

RECIPES

RECIPES

BREAKFAST

BREAKFAST

THE ULTIMATE SLOW COOKER BREAKFAST

Makes 2 servings
Preparation time – 8 minutes
Cooking time – 8 hours
Nutritional value per serving – 750 kcals,
47g carbs, 47g protein, 40g fat

INGREDIENTS

- ✔ 4 sausages
- ✔ 6 rashers of bacon
- ✔ 1 x 400g can chopped tomatoes
- ✔ 1 x 400g baked beans
- ✔ 4 eggs, beaten
- ✔ 100g button mushrooms
- ✔ 1 tbsp butter

METHOD

1. Just before you go to bed, start preparing your breakfast for the next day.

2. Place the sausages and bacon around the edges of the slow cooker, making sure each rasher of bacon is separated.

3. Add in the remaining ingredients in the order listed above before giving the mixture a stir to fully bring everything together.

4. Switch the slow cooker onto a low heat, add the lid, and leave it to cook through for 9 hours.

5. Once the 9 hours is up (and after a good night's sleep), switch off the slow cooker and serve up your breakfast!

BREAKFAST

STRAWBERRIES AND CREAM OVERNIGHT OATS

Makes 8 servings
Preparation time – 5 minutes
Cooking time – 8 hours
Nutritional value per serving – 243 kcals,
33g carbs, 12g protein, 4g fat

INGREDIENTS

- ✔ 200g rolled oats
- ✔ 500ml water
- ✔ 500ml milk (any type)
- ✔ 100g strawberries, hulled
- ✔ 150g Greek yoghurt

- ✔ 1 tbsp chia seeds
- ✔ 1 tsp dried cinnamon
- ✔ 1 tsp dried nutmeg

METHOD

1. Add all the ingredients into your slow cooker and mix them up until they form a consistent mixture.

2. Place the lid on your slow cooker and switch it onto a low heat.

3. Add the lid and cook for 6-8 hours.

4. Wake up the next day and serve up your oats! For an extra touch of flavour, add some additional strawberries, chia seeds, and cinnamon to the top of your oats.

BREAKFAST

CHIA SEED JAM OVERNIGHT OATS

Makes 8 servings
Preparation time – 15 minutes
Cooking time – 8 hours
Nutritional value per serving – 353 kcals,
52g carbs, 19g protein, 14g fat

INGREDIENTS

✔ 150g strawberries, hulled

✔ 3 tbsp chia seeds

✔ 3 tbsp flax seeds

✔ 3 tbsp sugar

✔ 200g rolled oats

✔ 800ml water

✔ 500ml milk (any type)

✔ 1 tsp dried cinnamon

METHOD

1. Grab a pan and add the strawberries. Cook them over a medium heat for 5 minutes until the fruit starts to break down.

2. Add in the chia seeds, flax seeds, and sugar, and stir until the ingredients are combined.

3. Continue to cook on a low heat for a further 2-3 minutes before removing the mixture and setting it aside in a bowl.

4. Place the remaining ingredients into the slow cooker, followed by the jam mixture.

5. Turn your slow cooker on, add the lid, and leave the chia seed jam overnight oats to cook on a low heat for around 8 hours until the next morning.

6. Serve up in a bowl with some added berries and an extra sprinkle of cinnamon on top.

SLOW COOKER FRENCH TOAST

Makes 8 servings
Preparation time – 20 minutes
Cooking time – 3 hours
Nutritional value per serving – 750 kcals,
47g carbs, 47g protein, 40g fat

BREAKFAST

INGREDIENTS

- ✔ 180g brioche loaf, cut into 1-inch cubes
- ✔ 1 tbsp unsalted butter
- ✔ 8 eggs, beaten
- ✔ 3 tbsp sugar
- ✔ 2 tsp vanilla extract
- ✔ 1 tsp ground cinnamon
- ✔ 1 tsp ground cumin

METHOD

1. Grease the inner component of your slow cooker with some butter or line with parchment paper.

2. In a bowl, whisk together all the ingredients, except the brioche loaf, until combined and transfer into the slow cooker.

3. Layer the bread evenly across the bottom of the slow cooker.

4. Pour the egg mixture evenly over the bread until it is fully covered.

5. Add the lid to the slow cooker and turn it onto a low heat. Cook for 6-8 hours.

6. Serve your French toast with a drizzle of syrup and some berries.

SLOW COOKER BREAKFAST SWEET POTATO BAKE

Makes 4 servings
Preparation time – 10 minutes
Cooking time – 8 hours
Nutritional value per serving – 645 kcals,
65g carbs, 29g protein, 22g fat

INGREDIENTS

- ✔ 300g sweet potato
- ✔ 1 x 400g can chopped tomatoes
- ✔ 1 x 400g can butter beans
- ✔ 2 rashers bacon, chopped
- ✔ 200ml milk (any type)
- ✔ 30g cheese

METHOD

1. Peel and chop your sweet potatoes and add them to your slow cooker.

2. Add the remaining ingredients, except the cheese, to the slow cooker.

3. Turn the slow cooker on to a low heat and cover with the lid.

4. The next morning, grate your cheese and add it into the slow cooker.

5. Leave to cook for an additional 10-15 minutes until the cheese has melted into the mixture before serving up for breakfast.

BREAKFAST

PEANUT BUTTER AND JAM SLOW COOKED OATS

Makes 4 servings
Preparation time – 5 minutes
Cooking time – 8 hours
Nutritional value per serving – 435 kcals,
59g carbs, 34g protein, 27g fat

INGREDIENTS

- ✔ 300g rolled oats
- ✔ 500ml water
- ✔ 500ml milk (any type)
- ✔ 2 tbsp strawberry jam
- ✔ 2 tbsp peanut butter
- ✔ 1 tsp dried ginger
- ✔ 1 tsp dried cinnamon

METHOD

1. Just before you head to bed, start preparing your slow cooked oats. Firstly, mix the oats in a large bowl with the water and milk.

2. Pour this mixture into the slow cooker before adding the remaining ingredients.

3. Turn the slow cooker onto a low heat, cover the mixture with the lid, and leave the cook on a gentle simmer for 6-8 hours.

4. When you get up the next morning, turn off the slow cooker, give the mixture a stir, and scoop a serving into a bowl. Top with an extra dash of peanut butter or jam if you wish.

BREAKFAST

SLOW COOKER CHEESE AND HAM CASSEROLE

Makes 4 servings
Preparation time – 10 minutes
Cooking time – 8 hours
Nutritional value per serving – 544 kcals,
16g carbs, 34g protein, 40g fat

INGREDIENTS

- ✔ 8 eggs, beaten
- ✔ 200ml milk (any type)
- ✔ 1 tsp salt
- ✔ ½ tsp pepper
- ✔ 200g ham, pre-cooked and chopped
- ✔ 50g cheddar cheese, grated

METHOD

1. Mix the eggs, milk, salt, and pepper in a bowl until fully combined.

2. Place half of the chopped ham at the bottom of the slow cooker and pour the egg mixture over it.

3. Top the mixture with the remaining ham before spreading the grated cheese evenly over the top of the mixture.

4. Turn the slow cooker onto a low heat, add the lid, and leave the casserole to cook overnight for at least 8 hours.

5. The next morning, switch off the slow cooker and allow the mixture to stand for 10 minutes. Serve up in your bowl and top with your favourite condiments.

BREAKFAST

SLOW COOKER COFFEE AND BANANA BAKED BRAN

Makes 4 servings
Preparation time – 10 minutes
Cooking time – 6-8 hours
Nutritional value per serving – 493 kcals,
43g carbs, 25g protein, 19g fat

INGREDIENTS

- ✔ 4 ripe bananas, and an extra ½ for toppings
- ✔ 500ml milk (any type)
- ✔ 200ml hot brewed coffee
- ✔ 2 tbsp brown sugar
- ✔ 2 tbsp chia seeds
- ✔ 200g high bran cereal
- ✔ 1 tsp vanilla extract
- ✔ 1 tsp dried cinnamon

METHOD

1. Mash up the bananas into heat-proof bowl and add the milk and coffee. Stir to fully combine the ingredients.

2. Add the remaining ingredients and stir until it forms a consistent mixture.

3. Pour the mixture into the slow cooker. Add some warm water until the machine is around three-quarters full.

4. Cover with the lid and turn the slow cooker onto a low heat and simmer overnight for at least 6 hours.

5. The next day, turn off the slow cooker and serve up your baked bran into a bowl. Top with the ½ sliced banana and a sprinkle of sugar.

SLOW COOKER APPLE AND CINNAMON ROLLS

Makes 8 servings
Preparation time – 10 minutes
Cooking time – 8 hours
Nutritional value per serving – 449 kcals,
63g carbs, 14g protein, 35g fat

INGREDIENTS

- ✔ 2 cinnamon rolls or cinnamon buns, chopped into quarters
- ✔ 2 apples, peeled and diced
- ✔ 4 eggs, beaten
- ✔ 150ml double cream
- ✔ 50g brown sugar
- ✔ 1 tsp vanilla extract
- ✔ 1 tsp cinnamon

METHOD

1. Grease the inside of your slow cooker and place the cinnamon roll pieces along the bottom.

2. Add the apples evenly around the rolls.

3. In a bowl, mix the eggs, cream, sugar, and vanilla extract until combined.

4. Pour the egg mixture over the rolls and sprinkle some cinnamon over the top.

5. Turn the slow cooker on to a low heat, put the lid on top, and leave to simmer until the next morning.

6. When you wake up, turn off the machine and serve up your slow cooker apple and cinnamon rolls. Add a touch more cinnamon to the top of your bowl for some extra flavour.

BREAKFAST

LUNCH

LUNCH

SLOW COOKER TURKEY CASSEROLE

Makes 4 servings
Preparation time – 15 minutes
Cooking time – 6 hours
Nutritional value per serving – 434 kcals,
42g carbs, 29g protein, 15g fat

LUNCH

INGREDIENTS

- ✔ 400g turkey breast, pre-cooked and chopped
- ✔ 1 onion, chopped
- ✔ ½ red pepper, sliced
- ✔ 4 eggs, beaten
- ✔ 200ml milk (any type)

- ✔ 2 tbsp plain flour
- ✔ 1 tsp dried chili flakes
- ✔ 30g cheddar cheese, grated

METHOD

1. After you've prepared all the ingredients, add the turkey, onion, and red pepper to the slow cooker.

2. In a bowl, whisk together the eggs, milk, flour, and chili flakes, and pour into the slow cooker so the mixture covers the turkey evenly.

3. Switch the slow cooker onto a low-medium heat, add the lid, and cook for 6 hours.

4. Once the turkey is soft and fully cooked, remove the lid, sprinkle the grated cheese across the mixture.

5. Place the lid back onto the machine and cook for a further 15 minutes or until the cheese has fully melted.

6. Turn off the slow cooker and serve up your turkey casserole.

SLOW COOKER CREAMY TOMATO SOUP

Makes 8 servings
Preparation time – 15 minutes
Cooking time – 2-3 hours
Nutritional value per serving – 230 kcals,
17g carbs, 9g protein, 17g fat

INGREDIENTS

- ✔ 1 tbsp olive oil
- ✔ 1 onion, chopped
- ✔ 2 cloves garlic, peeled and crushed
- ✔ 1 yellow pepper, sliced
- ✔ 1 stick celery, finely chopped
- ✔ 200g fresh beef tomatoes, quartered
- ✔ ½ x 400g can chopped tomatoes
- ✔ 1 tsp brown sugar
- ✔ 1 tsp black pepper
- ✔ 1 tsp dried herbs

METHOD

1. Heat the olive oil in a frying pan.

2. Add the onions and garlic. Cook on a medium heat for 8-10 until the onions have softened and caramelised.

3. Place the onions and garlic into the slow cooker along with the rest of the ingredients.

4. Add the lid and cook for 2-3 hours.

5. Transfer the soup to a blender or food processor and pulse until the mixture is smooth and consistent. This should only take a couple of minutes.

6. Pour a portion of soup into a bowl and top with some extra herbs or cheese. Enjoy it with your favourite crusty bread rolls!

LUNCH

SLOW COOKER MEXICAN BAKE

Makes 6-8 servings
Preparation time – 15 minutes
Cooking time – 4 hours
Nutritional value per serving – 450 kcals,
35g carbs, 24g protein, 12g fat

INGREDIENTS

- ✔ 2 cubes vegetable stock
- ✔ 200g quinoa, dry and uncooked
- ✔ 1 x 400g can kidney beans
- ✔ 1 x 400g can pinto beans
- ✔ 1 x 400g chopped tomatoes
- ✔ 1 onion, finely sliced
- ✔ 1 red pepper, finely sliced
- ✔ 1 tsp dried herbs
- ✔ 1 tsp black pepper
- ✔ 30g cheese (any type), grated

METHOD

1. Dissolve the stock cubes in boiling water according to the packet instructions. Pour the stock into the slow cooker.

2. Add the remaining ingredients, except the cheese.

3. Switch the slow cooker on, add the lid, and cook the ingredients for at least 4 hours until the quinoa is fully cooked. Most of the stock should have been absorbed and the mixture should be thick.

4. Sprinkle the cheese evenly over the top, add the lid, and cook for a further 10-15 minutes until the cheese has melted.

5. Serve up and add some extra cheese and pepper if desired.

LUNCH

VEGAN SLOW COOKER 'NO CHICKEN' CASSEROLE

Makes 8 servings
Preparation time – 20 minutes
Cooking time – 3-4 hours
Nutritional value per serving – 299 kcals,
15g carbs, 27g protein, 17g fat

INGREDIENTS

- ✔ 1 x 400g block extra-firm tofu
- ✔ 1 onion, chopped
- ✔ 1 carrot, peeled and chopped
- ✔ 1 leek, chopped
- ✔ 2 tsp brown sugar
- ✔ 1 x 400g can coconut milk
- ✔ 1 x 400g can chopped tomatoes
- ✔ 1 tsp curry powder
- ✔ 1 tsp chilli powder
- ✔ 1 tsp black pepper

METHOD

1. Drain the tofu and place the block on some clean paper towels. Place a heavy plate on top of the block to press the tofu down for 10-15 minutes. This removes the excess water. Alternatively, you can use a tofu press if you have one.

2. While the tofu is being pressed, add the remaining ingredients to the slow cooker. Add the tofu once it is firm enough.

3. Place the lid on top of the slow cooker and turn it onto a low to medium heat. Cook for 3-4 hours.

4. Serve up your no-meat casserole and enjoy!

SLOW COOKER CHICKEN NOODLE SOUP

Makes 8 servings
Preparation time – 15 minutes
Cooking time – 6 hours
Nutritional value per serving – 478 kcals,
20g carbs, 36g protein, 8g fat

INGREDIENTS

- ✔ 2 chicken stock cubes
- ✔ 500g boneless chicken breast, chopped
- ✔ 1 onion, chopped
- ✔ 1 clove garlic, peeled and crushed
- ✔ 2 carrots, peeled and chopped
- ✔ 1 leek, chopped
- ✔ 50g mange tout
- ✔ 1 tsp dried herbs
- ✔ 4 nests dry noodles

METHOD

1. Dissolve the chicken stock cubes in the required amount of boiling water as stated on the packet and pour into the slow cooker.

2. Add the remaining ingredients, except the noodles, and stir to combine.

3. Place the lid on the cooker and turn onto a low to medium heat. Cook for 6 hours.

4. Around 15 minutes before the 6 hours is complete, boil some water in a pan and cook the noodles for 10-12 minutes until soft.

5. Serve the noodles up into your bowls and pour the chicken broth mixture on top.

LUNCH

VEGAN SLOW COOKER TOFU AND VEGETABLE CASSEROLE

Makes 8 servings
Preparation time – 20 minutes
Cooking time – 2 hours
Nutritional value per serving – 379 kcals,
25g carbs, 30g protein, 11g fat

INGREDIENTS

- ✔ 2 vegetable stock cubes
- ✔ 1 x 400g block extra-firm tofu, diced
- ✔ 1 tbsp olive oil
- ✔ 1 onion, chopped
- ✔ 1 red pepper, sliced
- ✔ 2 leeks, sliced
- ✔ 3 carrots, peeled and chopped
- ✔ 1 courgette, chopped
- ✔ 1 tsp paprika
- ✔ 1 tsp dried herbs

METHOD

1. Drain the tofu and place the block on some clean paper towels. Place a heavy plate on top of the block to press the tofu down for 10-15 minutes. Alternatively, you can use a tofu press if you have one.

2. In the meantime, boil enough water to fully dissolve the vegetable stock cubes. Add the stock to your slow cooker.

3. Heat the olive oil in a frying pan and cook the onion, pepper, and leeks for 8-10 minutes until they are softened.

4. Add the onion mixture to the slow cooker along with the pressed tofu, carrots, courgettes, paprika, and dried herbs.

5. Place the lid on top of the machine and switch to a moderate heat. Cook for 2-3 hours until the tofu is fully cooked, and the vegetables are soft.

6. Serve up in a bowl and enjoy!

LUNCH

SLOW COOKER TEMPEH NOODLE SOUP

Makes 4 servings
Preparation time – 10 minutes
Cooking time – 4 hours
Nutritional value per serving – 346 kcals,
29g carbs, 31g protein, 14g fat

INGREDIENTS

- ✔ 1 tbsp coconut oil
- ✔ 1 onion, sliced
- ✔ 2 vegetable stock cubes
- ✔ 1 x 400g block tempeh, diced
- ✔ 2 carrots, peeled and chopped
- ✔ 100g baby sweetcorn
- ✔ 100g mange tout
- ✔ 4 nests wholewheat noodles
- ✔ 1 tsp salt
- ✔ 1 tsp black pepper

METHOD

1. Heat the coconut oil in a frying pan and add the onion. Cook over a medium heat for 8-10 minutes until it softens and becomes fragrant.

2. Dissolve the vegetable stock cubes in boiling water according to the packet instructions and pour this into the slow cooker.

3. Place the onions in the slow cooker along with all the remaining ingredients, except the noodles, salt, and pepper.

4. Boil some water in a pan and add the noodles. Cook for 10-12 minutes until soft and transfer into the slow cooker.

5. Switch the machine onto a medium heat, add the lid, and cook for 4 hours until the ingredients have softened and most of the stock has been absorbed.

6. Once ready, serve up into 4 even portions and add a sprinkle of salt and pepper to each dish.

LUNCH

SLOW COOKER CHICKEN GNOCCHI SOUP

Makes 4 servings
Preparation time – 15 minutes
Cooking time – 4 hours
Nutritional value per serving – 338 kcals,
40g carbs, 23g protein, 7g fat

LUNCH

INGREDIENTS

- ✔ 400g boneless chicken breast, pre-cooked and sliced
- ✔ 1 onion, sliced
- ✔ 1 stick celery, sliced
- ✔ 1 carrot, chopped
- ✔ 1 tsp dried basil
- ✔ 1 tsp dried oregano

- ✔ 2 chicken stock cubes
- ✔ 3 tbsp corn starch, dissolved in 2 tbsp water
- ✔ 1 x 400g packet pre-cooked gnocchi
- ✔ 1 tsp salt

METHOD

1. Place the chicken, onion, celery, carrot, and herbs in the slow cooker, add the lid, and cook on a low heat for 3 hours.

2. Dissolve the stock cubes in the amount of boiling water specified on the packet and pour this into the slow cooker.

3. Add the corn starch, gnocchi, and a dash of salt, cover with the lid once again, and allow the mixture to cook for a further 45 minutes to 1 hour.

4. Serve when the soup has thickened, and the chicken is fully cooked. Enjoy with a side of crusty bread and butter.

SLOW COOKER VEGGIE OMELETTE

Makes 8 servings
Preparation time – 10 minutes
Cooking time – 1-2 hours
Nutritional value per serving – 197 kcals,
14g carbs, 19g protein, 10g fat

INGREDIENTS

- ✔ 8 eggs, beaten
- ✔ 100ml milk (any type)
- ✔ 50g parmesan cheese, grated
- ✔ 1 tsp dried herbs
- ✔ 1 tsp chili powder
- ✔ 1 onion, sliced
- ✔ 1 yellow pepper, sliced

METHOD

1. Grease the inner compartment of the slow cooker using butter or oil.

2. Combine the eggs, milk, cheese, and seasoning in a bowl and whisk until combined.

3. Add this mixture to the slow cooker along with the onions and pepper.

4. Place the lid on the slow cooker and turn it on to a high heat. Cook for 1-2 hours until the eggs are fully cooked.

5. A couple of minutes before the 1-2 hours is complete, add a sprinkle more cheese on top of the omelettes and cook for a further few minutes until the additional cheese has melted.

6. Serve up with your favourite garnish and enjoy.

LUNCH

SLOW COOKER BUTTERNUT SQUASH SOUP

Makes 8 servings
Preparation time – 15 minutes
Cooking time – 6-8 hours
Nutritional value per serving – 280 kcals,
16g carbs, 6g protein, 9g fat

LUNCH

INGREDIENTS

- ✔ 1 tbsp oil
- ✔ 1 onion, chopped
- ✔ 1 butternut squash, peeled and cubed
- ✔ 2 vegetable stock cubes
- ✔ ½ tsp black pepper
- ✔ ½ tsp dried garlic granules

METHOD

1. Heat the oil in a frying pan and cook the onion for 8-10 minutes until it is lightly browned and fragrant.

2. Add the onions to the slow cooker along with the remaining ingredients.

3. Pour 400ml water into the slow cooker.

4. Cover with the lid and cook on a low heat for 6-8 hours.

5. Once cooked, remove the soup from the slow cooker.

6. Place half of the soup from the slow cooker and place in a blender. Pulse until the mixture is smooth and creamy.

7. Combine the two halves of the soup once again and stir to mix the non-blended and the blended halves evenly together.

8. Serve the soup warm in a bowl alongside some crusty bread and enjoy!

LUNCH

SLOW COOKER SWEET AND STICKY CHICKEN WINGS

Makes 4 servings
Preparation time – 5 minutes
Cooking time – 6 hours
Nutritional value per serving – 387 kcals,
22g carbs, 21g protein, 16g fat

LUNCH

INGREDIENTS

- ✔ 2 tbsp soy sauce
- ✔ 2 tbsp balsamic vinegar
- ✔ 3 tbsp honey
- ✔ 1 tsp hot sauce
- ✔ Zest 1 lemon or lime
- ✔ 600g chicken wings
- ✔ 4 tbsp corn starch
- ✔ 1 tbsp sesame seeds
- ✔ 1 tbsp dried mixed herbs

METHOD

1. Mix the soy sauce, balsamic vinegar, honey, hot sauce, and lemon or lime zest in a bowl until fully combined.

2. Place the chicken wings in your slow cooker and pour the wet mixture over the top. Stir until all the wings are fully covered.

3. Add the lid to the slow cooker and cook the wings on a low heat for 6 hours.

4. In a bowl, mix the corn starch with 1 tbsp water and stir to combine. Add this into the slow cooker 10 minutes before the 6 hours is complete.

5. Remove the chicken wings from the slow cooker and coat in the sesame seeds and dried mixed herbs.

6. Serve up the chicken wings along with a side of chips or salad.

LUNCH

SUCCULENT SLOW COOKER PULLED PORK

Makes 8 servings
Preparation time – 10 minutes
Cooking time – 6 hours
Nutritional value per serving – 411 kcals,
27g carbs, 30g protein, 19g fat

LUNCH

INGREDIENTS

- ✔ 1 onion, finely chopped
- ✔ 4 tbsp ketchup
- ✔ 3 tbsp tomato paste
- ✔ 3 tbsp BBQ sauce
- ✔ 2 tbsp apple cider vinegar
- ✔ 1 tbsp BBQ seasoning
- ✔ 1 tsp smoked paprika
- ✔ 1 tsp garlic powder
- ✔ 1 tsp mustard powder
- ✔ 600g pork, excess fat removed
- ✔ ½ tsp salt
- ✔ ½ tsp black pepper

METHOD

1. Combine the onion, ketchup, tomato paste, BBQ sauce, apple cider vinegar, and spices in a bowl until combined.

2. Chop the pork into pieces and rub each piece into the sauce mixture until fully covered.

3. Add the pork to the slow cooker along with a pinch of salt and black pepper

4. Cover with the lid and cook on a high heat for 6-8 hours until the pork is cooked through.

5. Remove the pork from the slow cooker and shred.

6. Serve in a bun along with some salad and extra BBQ sauce.

DINNER

SLOW COOKER BEEF AND VEGETABLE STEW

Makes 4 servings
Preparation time – 15 minutes
Cooking time – 5 hours
Nutritional value per serving – 564 kcals,
35g carbs, 39g protein, 24g fat

INGREDIENTS

- ✔ 2 tbsp olive oil
- ✔ 1 onion, chopped
- ✔ ½ spring onion, chopped
- ✔ 1 clove garlic, chopped
- ✔ 2 large carrots, chopped into small chunks
- ✔ 1 large leek, chopped finely
- ✔ 2 celery sticks, chopped finely
- ✔ ½ can chopped tomatoes
- ✔ 2 tbsp tomato puree
- ✔ Handful fresh thyme
- ✔ Handful fresh parsley
- ✔ 2 beef stock cubes, crushed
- ✔ 800g beef, diced

METHOD

1. Heat 1 tbsp oil in a frying pan and add the onion, spring onion, and garlic. Cook them until the onions start to caramelise. This should take about 5-6 minutes.

2. Add the carrots, leek, and celery and continue cooking for a few minutes.

3. Transfer this mixture into the slow cooker machine along with the chopped tomatoes, tomato puree, fresh herbs, and beef stock cubes.

4. Heat the remaining tablespoon of oil in the frying pan and add the beef. Cook until it is cooked through.

5. Transfer the beef to the slow cooker and add enough water to fill the slow cooker by a half to two-thirds.

6. Leave the mixture to cook for 5 hours, stirring occasionally.

7. Once the dish is ready, serve up and enjoy!

DINNER

SLOW COOKER CHICKEN CASSEROLE

Makes 4 servings
Preparation time – 15 minutes
Cooking time – 6 hours
Nutritional value per serving – 402 kcals,
35g carbs, 45g protein, 8g fat

INGREDIENTS

- ✔ 2 tbsp olive oil
- ✔ 1 onion, chopped
- ✔ 1 clove garlic, chopped
- ✔ 500g boneless chicken breast, diced
- ✔ 1 potato, chopped into small chunks
- ✔ 2 large carrots, cut into small chunks
- ✔ 1 courgette, chopped into small chunks
- ✔ 1 large leek, chopped finely
- ✔ 2 tbsp Dijon mustard
- ✔ 2 tbsp tomato puree
- ✔ 2 chicken stock cubes, crushed

METHOD

1. Heat 1 tbsp oil in a frying pan and add the onion and garlic. Cook for 8-10 minutes until the onions start to turn brown and caramelise.

2. Set the onions and garlic aside before heating the remaining tablespoon of oil in the pan and cooking the chicken for 5-6 minutes until it starts to brown.

3. Transfer the onions, garlic, and chicken into your slow cooker and add the remaining ingredients.

4. Add some water to the pot until it is half full.

5. Cover with a lid and leave to simmer for around 6 hours.

6. Once it is ready, remove and dish into 4 portions.

DINNER

SLOW COOKER BEEF TACOS

Makes 8 servings
Preparation time – 10 minutes
Cooking time – 4-5 hours
Nutritional value per serving – 365 kcals,
25g carbs, 21g protein, 17g fat

INGREDIENTS

- ✔ 1 x 400g can chopped tomatoes
- ✔ 1 tbsp chipotle sauce
- ✔ 2 tsp ground cumin
- ✔ ½ tsp salt
- ✔ 3 cloves garlic, peeled and finely chopped
- ✔ 1 onion, thinly sliced
- ✔ 400g beef, minced

METHOD

1. Combine the chopped tomatoes, chipotle sauce, cumin, and salt in a bowl until fully mixed.

2. Stir in the garlic, onion, and beef.

3. Transfer the mixture into the slow cooker, cover with the lid, and cook on a high heat for 4-5 hours until the beef is cooked.

4. Serve up in some tortillas or taco shells alongside some grated cheese, sour cream, salsa, and guacamole.

SLOW COOKER TOFU TIKKA MASALA

Makes 4 servings
Preparation time – 20 minutes
Cooking time – 3-4 hours
Nutritional value per serving – 376 kcals,
29g carbs, 38g protein, 10g fat

INGREDIENTS

- ✔ 1 x 400g block extra-firm tofu
- ✔ 1 tbsp coconut oil
- ✔ 1 tsp cumin seeds
- ✔ 1 tbsp garam masala
- ✔ 1 tbsp curry powder
- ✔ 1 tbsp paprika
- ✔ 1 tsp black pepper
- ✔ 1 tsp salt
- ✔ 1 onion, chopped
- ✔ 2 cloves garlic, peeled and crushed
- ✔ 1 red pepper, sliced
- ✔ 2 green chili peppers, finely chopped
- ✔ 5 tbsp tomato paste
- ✔ 1 x 400g can chopped tomatoes
- ✔ 1 tbsp brown sugar
- ✔ Handful fresh coriander

METHOD

1. Drain the tofu by placing it on some clean paper towels to remove any excess water. Place a heavy plate on top of the block to press the tofu down for 10-15 minutes. Alternatively, you can use a tofu press if you have one.

2. Heat the coconut oil in a large wok or frying pan and add the cumin seeds. Cook for 1-2 minutes before adding all the spices and the salt. Stir for another minute or until the seeds become fragrant.

3. Add the onion, garlic, peppers, and tomato paste and cook for a further 2 minutes.

4. Add the canned chopped tomatoes into the pan and give the mixture a good stir.

5. Next, place the tofu in the pan along with the sugar and stir to combine them with the other ingredients.

6. Transfer the contents of the pan into your slow cooker and place the lid on top.

7. Cook on a medium heat for 3-4 hours.

8. Once cooked, serve up in a bowl and top with fresh coriander and eat with some basmati rice and poppadoms.

SLOW COOKER CHICKEN LASAGNE

Makes 4 servings
Preparation time – 15 minutes
Cooking time – 4 hours
Nutritional value per serving – 654 kcals,
43g carbs, 34g protein, 28g fat

INGREDIENTS

- ✔ 1 tbsp coconut oil
- ✔ 1 onion, sliced
- ✔ 1 garlic clove, peeled and crushed
- ✔ 1 x 400g jar Alfredo sauce
- ✔ 400g boneless chicken breast, pre-cooked and diced
- ✔ 1 x 400g can chopped tomatoes
- ✔ 6 tbsp tomato paste
- ✔ 8 sheets lasagne
- ✔ 75g cheddar cheese, grated

METHOD

1. Heat the oil in a frying pan and add the onion and garlic. Cook for 8-10 minutes until they become fragrant.

2. Spread a quarter layer of Alfredo sauce across the bottom of the slow cooker, followed by a quarter of the onion and garlic mix, and 100g of chicken.

3. Layer 2 lasagne sheets over the top, followed by a third of the canned chopped tomatoes and 2 tbsp tomato paste.

4. Repeat steps 2 and 3 until all the ingredients have been used, with the final layer should being 2 lasagne sheets.

5. Turn the slow cooker on to a low heat and cook for 4 hours with the lid on. Around 15 minutes before the 4 hours are complete, sprinkle most of the grated cheese evenly on top of the lasagne.

6. Serve up with some chips or salad and top with the remaining cheese.

DINNER

SLOW COOKER CHICKPEA, SWEET POTATO, AND SPINACH CURRY

Makes 4 servings
Preparation time – 15 minutes
Cooking time – 4 hours
Nutritional value per serving – 369 kcals,
45g carbs, 20g protein, 14g fat

INGREDIENTS

- ✔ 1 tbsp olive oil
- ✔ 1 onion, sliced
- ✔ 1 x 400g can chickpeas, drained and rinsed
- ✔ 2 tbsp curry powder
- ✔ 200g sweet potato, peeled and diced
- ✔ 1 bell pepper, sliced
- ✔ 1 x 400g can chopped tomatoes
- ✔ 1 x 200g can coconut milk
- ✔ 2 cloves garlic, peeled and chopped
- ✔ 1 tsp salt
- ✔ 4 handful fresh spinach

METHOD

1. Place the oil, onion, chickpeas, and curry powder in the slow cooker and stir to mix everything together.

2. Add the remaining ingredients, except the spinach on top. Do not stir. Leave the chickpeas at the bottom of the slow cooker.

3. Add the lid to the slow cooker and cook for 4 hours. The mixture should now be smooth and soup-like. The chickpeas should be slightly softened.

4. Add the spinach and cover with the lid again. Cook for a further 15 minutes until the spinach has wilted.

5. Stir the curry to mix the chickpeas with the sweet potato and spinach, and serve up with some rice, poppadoms, and naan bread.

SMOKY BBQ SLOW COOKER TEMPEH AND SWEET POTATO

Makes 4 servings
Preparation time – 25 minutes
Cooking time – 4 hours
Nutritional value per serving – 496 kcals,
39g carbs, 34g protein, 17g fat

INGREDIENTS

- ✔ 1 x 400g block tempeh, diced
- ✔ 2 tbsp BBQ sauce
- ✔ 2 tbsp olive oil
- ✔ 1 onion, sliced
- ✔ 1 yellow pepper, sliced
- ✔ 100g green beans, chopped
- ✔ 2 tsp cumin
- ✔ 2 tsp smoked paprika
- ✔ 2 tsp BBQ seasoning
- ✔ 400g sweet potato, peeled and diced
- ✔ 2 vegetable stock cubes

METHOD

1. Coat the tempeh in the BBQ sauce and leave the marinade for 15 minutes.

2. In the meantime, heat the olive oil in a large frying pan and add the onion, pepper, green beans, and spices. Cook for 10 minutes until the vegetables have softened and the onions start to caramelise.

3. Remove the onion mixture from the pan and add the BBQ tempeh. Cook for 10 minutes until the tempeh has browned a little on each side.

4. Add the onion mixture, tempeh, and sweet potato to your slow cooker.

5. Dissolve the stock cubes in boiling water according to the packet instructions and pour over the ingredients in the slow cooker.

6. Add the lid and turn on the slow cooker to a medium heat.

7. Cook for 4 hours before plating up in 4 servings.

DINNER

SLOW COOKER PIZZA PASTA BAKE

Makes 8 servings
Preparation time – 20 minutes
Cooking time – 3 hours
Nutritional value per serving – 545 kcals,
34g carbs, 29g protein, 28g fat

INGREDIENTS

- ✔ 2 tbsp olive oil
- ✔ 400g ground beef
- ✔ 1 onion, chopped
- ✔ 1 clove garlic, peeled and finely sliced
- ✔ 1 x 400g can chopped tomatoes
- ✔ 4 tbsp tomato paste
- ✔ 400g uncooked pasta (any type)
- ✔ 100g cheddar cheese, grated

METHOD

1. In a large frying pan, heat the olive oil and cook the beef until it starts to turn brown. There should be no pink area left.

2. Add the onion and garlic and cook for a further 10 minutes until the vegetables have softened.

3. Add the chopped tomatoes and the tomato paste to the frying pan and stir the ingredients until well combined.

4. Cook the pasta according to the packet instructions.

5. Add the beef mixture and the pasta to the slow cooker and mix well.

6. Stir in half of the cheese, add the lid to the slow cooker, and turn it onto a medium heat.

7. Cook for 3 hours until fully heated through.

8. Serve into 8 portions and top each one with the remaining grated cheese.

DINNER

SLOW COOKER RATATOUILLE

Makes 4 servings
Preparation time – 15 minutes
Cooking time – 3 hours
Nutritional value per serving – 299 kcals,
28g carbs, 19g protein, 8g fat

INGREDIENTS

- ✔ 150g white potato
- ✔ 1 onion, sliced
- ✔ 2 cloves garlic, peeled and crushed
- ✔ 2 courgettes, sliced
- ✔ 1 red pepper, sliced
- ✔ 1 zucchini, sliced
- ✔ 1 x 400g can chopped tomatoes or tomato pasta sauce
- ✔ 2 tsp dried herbs
- ✔ 4 tbsp cheese (any type), grated

METHOD

1. Add all the ingredients into the slow cooker and mix until they are fully combined.

2. Add the lid to the slow cooker and turn it onto a medium heat.

3. Cook for 3 hours until the potatoes are soft.

4. Serve up, top with some grated cheese, and enjoy with a roll of crispy bread and butter.

DINNER

CHICKEN POT PIE SLOW COOKER EDITION

Makes 8 servings
Preparation time – 25 minutes
Cooking time – 4 hours
Nutritional value per serving – 457 kcals,
38g carbs, 29g protein, 15g fat

INGREDIENTS

- ✔ 2 cubes chicken stock
- ✔ 4 boneless chicken breasts
- ✔ 1 x 400g can chicken and vegetable soup
- ✔ 1 onion, sliced
- ✔ 2 carrots
- ✔ 1 stick celery, sliced
- ✔ 1 tsp dried herbs
- ✔ 1 tsp paprika
- ✔ 1 tsp salt
- ✔ 1 tsp pepper
- ✔ 100g frozen mixed vegetables
- ✔ 8 large biscuits

METHOD

1. Dissolve the chicken stock cubes in boiling water according to the packet instructions.

2. Add the stock to the slow cooker alongside the soup, onion, carrots, celery, herbs, spices, and salt.

3. Place the lid on top of the slow cooker and cook on a low heat for 4 hours.

4. Around 30 minutes prior to the 4-hour mark, add the mixed vegetables to the slow cooker.

5. In the meantime, bake the biscuits according to the directions on the packet.

6. Once the slow cooker ingredients are cooked, serve into 8 bowls, and sprinkle the biscuits on top. Serve up with some baked potatoes and a side of cooked vegetables.

DINNER

SLOW COOKER LENTIL CURRY

Makes 4 servings
Preparation time – 10 minutes
Cooking time – 6-8 hours
Nutritional value per serving – 359 kcals,
24g carbs, 18g protein, 16g fat

INGREDIENTS

- 200g dry lentils (any colour)
- 1 onion, sliced
- 1 clove garlic, peeled and crushed
- 1 tbsp dried ginger
- 1 tbsp dried cumin
- 1 tsp dried turmeric
- 1 x 400g can chopped tomatoes
- ½ x 400g can coconut milk
- Handful fresh coriander

METHOD

1. Combine all of the ingredients except the coconut milk, and coriander, and place them into the slow cooker. Pour in 500ml water or enough to soak the lentils.

2. Add the lid and turn the slow cooker onto a low heat.

3. Cook for 6-8 hours until the lentils have absorbed most of the water. Keep checking the mixture every hour or two and add more water if required.

4. Once the cooking is complete, turn off the slow cooker and stir in the coconut milk and fresh coriander.

5. Serve up with some basmati rice, poppadoms, and naan bread.

SIDES AND SNACKS

SLOW COOKER BLACK BEANS

Makes 8 servings
Preparation time – 10 minutes
Cooking time – 3 hours
Nutritional value per serving – 156 kcals,
25g carbs, 14g protein, 4g fat

INGREDIENTS

- ✔ 400g dried black beans
- ✔ 1 onion, sliced
- ✔ 2 cloves garlic, peeled and sliced
- ✔ 500ml water
- ✔ 1 tsp black pepper

METHOD

1. Rinse the black beans and add them to the slow cooker.

2. Add the rest of the ingredients to the machine, place the lid on top, and cook for 3 hours on a medium to high heat, or until all the water has been absorbed by the black beans. The beans should be soft to touch.

3. Serve up as a side dish for the whole family to enjoy. Store any left overs in airtight containers in the refrigerator for up to 5 days.

SLOW COOKER MEXICAN RICE

Makes 8 servings
Preparation time – 10 minutes
Cooking time – 1-2 hours
Nutritional value per serving – 178 kcals,
28g carbs, 11g protein, 3g fat

INGREDIENTS

- ✔ 200g jasmine rice
- ✔ 1 vegetable stock cube
- ✔ 1 tsp mixed spices
- ✔ 1 tsp coriander
- ✔ 2 tbsp hot salsa
- ✔ 1 x 400g can black beans
- ✔ 2 tbsp cheese, grated

METHOD

1. Rinse the rice through a colander until the water runs clear. Place the rice in your slow cooker.

2. Dissolve the stock cube in the required amount of boiling water according to the packet instructions and pour over the rice.

3. Add the mixed spices, coriander, and salsa, cover with the lid, and cook on a medium heat for 1 hour.

4. Stir in the black beans and 1 tbsp cheese, re-cover with the lid, and cook for a further 30 minutes.

5. Once the beans have softened and most of the stock has been absorbed by the rice, serve up into 8 portions and top each serving evenly with the remaining cheese.

SIDES AND SNACKS

SLOW COOKER SWEET POTATO WEDGES

Makes 8 servings
Preparation time – 10 minutes
Cooking time – 4 hours
Nutritional value per serving – 282 kcals,
25g carbs, 7g protein, 5g fat

INGREDIENTS

- ✔ 600g sweet potato, cut into wedges
- ✔ 100g butter, melted
- ✔ 2 tbsp brown sugar
- ✔ 1 tsp cinnamon
- ✔ 1 tsp nutmeg
- ✔ 1 tsp black pepper

METHOD

1. Place your potato wedges in a bowl and pour over the melted butter. Stir until the potatoes are fully covered.

2. Sprinkle the sugar and spices over the top of the potatoes and toss until the seasoning is evenly spread across the potatoes.

3. Transfer the potatoes into your slow cooker, add the lid, and cook on a high heat for 4 hours until the potatoes are fully cooked through.

SLOW COOKER MASH POTATO

Makes 8 servings
Preparation time – 15 minutes
Cooking time – 1-2 hours
Nutritional value per serving – 215 kcals,
19g carbs, 7g protein, 15g fat

INGREDIENTS

- ✔ 500g new potatoes, halved
- ✔ 200ml milk (any type)
- ✔ 50g butter
- ✔ 50g sour cream
- ✔ 1 tsp salt
- ✔ ½ tsp black pepper

METHOD

1. Line the inner part of your slow cooker with parchment paper.

2. Place all the ingredients into the slow cooker along with 500ml water.

3. Cover with the lid and cook on a low heat for 1-2 hours, stirring every 30 minutes.

4. Once complete, remove from the slow cooker and serve up while still hot.

SLOW COOKER JASMINE RICE

Makes 8 servings
Preparation time – 10 minutes
Cooking time – 2 hours
Nutritional value per serving – 187 kcals,
21g carbs, 6g protein, 4g fat

INGREDIENTS

✔ 250g uncooked jasmine rice

✔ 500ml water

✔ ½ tbsp butter, melted

METHOD

1. Place all the ingredients into the slow cooker and stir until all the rice grains are covered.

2. Add the lid and cook on a low heat for 2 hours or until the water has been absorbed by the rice.

3. Serve as a side dish to your main meal.

SIDES AND SNACKS

TEXAS-STYLE SLOW COOKER BBQ BEANS

Makes 20 servings
Preparation time – 15 minutes
Cooking time – 4-6 hours
Nutritional value per serving – 276 kcals,
25g carbs, 15g protein, 21g fat

INGREDIENTS

- ✔ 1 tbsp olive oil
- ✔ 4 rashers bacon
- ✔ 1 x 400g can kidney beans, drained and rinsed
- ✔ 1 x 400g black beans, drained and rinsed
- ✔ 2 cloves garlic, peeled and chopped.
- ✔ 1 onion, chopped
- ✔ 2 tbsp brown sugar
- ✔ 3 tbsp BBQ sauce
- ✔ 1 tbsp mustard
- ✔ 1 tsp chili powder
- ✔ ½ tsp salt
- ✔ ½ tsp black pepper
- ✔ 2 tbsp cheddar cheese, grated

METHOD

1. Heat the oil in a frying pan and cook the bacon on a medium heat until fully cooked and crispy.

2. Set aside to drain on some paper towel for a few minutes before chopping into pieces.

3. Place all the ingredients into the slow cooker and stir to combine. If the mixture looks a little dry, add some water.

4. Cover with the lid and cook on a low heat for 4-6 hours until the beans have softened.

5. Serve up as a side to your main meal.

SLOW COOKER MIXED VEGETABLES

Makes 10 servings
Preparation time – 10 minutes
Cooking time – 4 hours
Nutritional value per serving – 70 kcals,
6g carbs, 10g protein, 7g fat

INGREDIENTS

- ✔ 1 cube vegetable stock
- ✔ 4 carrots, chopped
- ✔ 2 sticks celery, chopped
- ✔ 2 onions, chopped
- ✔ 100g green beans, chopped
- ✔ 1 green pepper, sliced

METHOD

1. Dissolve the vegetable stock cube in boiling water.

2. Pour the stock into the slow cooker and add the rest of the ingredients. Stir well to combine.

3. Place the lid on the slow cooker and cook the mixture for 4 hours on a medium heat.

SLOW COOKER MEATBALLS

Makes 10 servings
Preparation time – 10 minutes
Cooking time – 4 hours
Nutritional value per serving – 70 kcals,
6g carbs, 10g protein, 7g fat

INGREDIENTS

- ✔ 2 x 500g jars marinara sauce
- ✔ 500g ground beef
- ✔ 2 eggs, beaten
- ✔ 1 tbsp Worcestershire sauce
- ✔ 200g breadcrumbs
- ✔ 100g cheddar cheese, grated (optional)
- ✔ 1 tsp salt
- ✔ 1 tsp black pepper

METHOD

1. Combine all the ingredients in a mixing bowl minus the marinara sauce and use your hands to mix it fully.

2. Use your hands or a tablespoon to scoop out small individual bits of the mixture and roll them into golf-sized balls.

3. Place the meatballs on a lined baking tray and cook them in the oven on gas mark 6/200oC for 10 minutes until they have browned slightly.

4. Transfer the meatballs to your slow cooker and pour in the two jars of marinara sauce.

5. Mix to combine, add the lid, and cook for 4 hours on high.

6. Serve up in a side dish for the whole family to enjoy. Freeze any leftovers in an airtight container.

SLOW COOKER MIXED NUTS

Makes 10 servings
Preparation time – 10 minutes
Cooking time – 3 hours
Nutritional value per serving – 199 kcals,
13g carbs, 12g protein, 18g fat

INGREDIENTS

- ✔ 300g mixed nuts (almonds, cashews, pecans, walnuts, brazil nuts)
- ✔ 100g brown sugar
- ✔ 5 tbsp honey or maple syrup
- ✔ 1 tbsp cinnamon
- ✔ 2 tsp vanilla extract
- ✔ 50ml water

METHOD

1. Mix all the ingredients together in a bowl, except the water.

2. Place the nut mixture in the slow cooker and pour over the water until they are evenly coated.

3. Place the lid on the slow cooker and cook on low for 3 hours until the pecans are crisp and crunchy.

4. Serve as a snack for everybody to enjoy!

SIDES AND SNACKS

SLOW COOKER CHOCOLATE AND PEANUT BUTTER BITES

Makes 20 servings
Preparation time – 5 minutes
Cooking time – 2 hours
Nutritional value per serving – 231 kcals,
19g carbs, 8g protein, 15g fat

INGREDIENTS

- ✔ 400g unsalted peanuts, chopped
- ✔ 400g milk chocolate
- ✔ 100g chocolate chips
- ✔ 400g peanut butter
- ✔ 2 tbsp honey or maple syrup

METHOD

1. Grease the inner compartment of your slow cooker.

2. Mix all the ingredients together in a large bowl and transfer into the slow cooker.

3. Place the lid onto the machine and turn it onto a low heat. Cook for 2 hours, stirring once every 30 minutes.

4. Remove the sweet and sticky mixture in small clusters using a spoon and place them on a baking sheet.

5. Allow the clusters to cool for 1-2 hours. Store in the fridge or freezer.

SIDES AND SNACKS

SLOW COOKER BELL PEPPER AND CORN

Makes 6 servings
Preparation time – 10 minutes
Cooking time – 2 hours
Nutritional value per serving – 123 kcals,
29g carbs, 12g protein, 18g fat

INGREDIENTS

- ✔ 1 x 400g can sweetcorn
- ✔ 1 red bell pepper, sliced
- ✔ 2 tbsp sour cream
- ✔ 50g cheese (any type), grated
- ✔ 100g cream cheese
- ✔ 2 tbsp fresh chives, chopped

METHOD

1. Mix the corn, pepper, sour cream, and cheese in a bowl and transfer into the slow cooker.

2. Add the lid onto the machine and cook on a low heat for 2 hours.

3. After 2 hours, stir in the cream cheese until the corn is fully covered.

4. Cook for a further 15 minutes.

5. Once cooked, serve the corn with some fresh chives sprinkled on top.

DESSERTS

DESSERTS

SLOW COOKER CHOCOLATE FUDGE

Makes 20 servings
Preparation time – 5 minutes
Cooking time – 2 hours
Nutritional value per serving – 176 kcals,
15g carbs, 8g protein, 13g fat

INGREDIENTS

- ✔ 150g milk chocolate
- ✔ 100g chocolate chips
- ✔ 1 tsp vanilla extract
- ✔ 1 tbsp salted butter

METHOD

1. Grease the inner compartment of the slow cooker with a little bit of oil.

2. Add all the ingredients into the slow cooker and stir to combine.

3. Place the lid onto the machine and cook the ingredients on low for 2 hours, stirring every 30 minutes.

4. Once cooked, remove the mixture, and leave to cool in a baking tray for 10 minutes.

5. Transfer the fudge into the fridge to store for at least 4 hours, after which you can cut it into bite-sized pieces.

TRIPLE CHOCOLATE SLOW COOKER BROWNIES

Makes 20 servings
Preparation time – 15 minutes
Cooking time – 3 hours
Nutritional value per serving – 312 kcals,
30g carbs, 12g protein, 26g fat

INGREDIENTS

- ✔ 300g plain flour
- ✔ 150g cocoa powder
- ✔ ½ tsp baking powder
- ✔ 75g unsalted butter
- ✔ 100g milk chocolate
- ✔ 100g dark chocolate
- ✔ 100g sugar
- ✔ 3 eggs, beaten
- ✔ 1 tsp vanilla extract
- ✔ 100g white chocolate chips

METHOD

1. Lightly grease the inner compartment of your slow cooker or use parchment paper to line it.

2. In a bowl, whisk together the flour, cocoa powder, and baking powder.

3. Place the butter, milk chocolate, and dark chocolate in a large pan and lightly heat until melted.

4. Turn off the heat and pour the sugar into the butter and chocolate mix, followed by the eggs, vanilla, and chocolate chips.

5. Stir the flour mixture into the pan until fully combined. Transfer into the slow cooker and smooth out the top of the mixture so it is even.

6. Place the lid on the slow cooker and cook the brownie mixture on a low heat for 3 hours.

7. Once complete, remove from the slow cooker and leave to cool on a drying rack before cutting into squares.

8. Store in the fridge.

DESSERTS

SLOW COOKER CHOCOLATE CARAMEL CAKE

Makes 8 servings
Preparation time – 10 minutes
Cooking time – 6 hours
Nutritional value per serving – 576 kcals,
49g carbs, 8g protein, 42g fat

INGREDIENTS

- ✔ 1 x 400g can condensed milk
- ✔ 200g plain flour
- ✔ 100g sugar
- ✔ 3 tbsp cocoa powder
- ✔ 1 tsp baking powder
- ✔ 200ml milk (any type)
- ✔ 3 tbsp olive oil
- ✔ 1 tsp vanilla extract
- ✔ 150g milk chocolate, chopped
- ✔ 100ml double cream

METHOD

1. Remove the label from your condensed milk can and place in a stockpot.

2. Fill the stockpot with around 2 inches of water and bring to a boil. Simmer for 3 hours to caramelise the milk.

3. Grease the inner component of the slow cooker or line it with parchment paper.

4. In a bowl, whisk the flour, sugar, cocoa powder, and baking powder until fully combined.

5. Add the milk, olive oil, vanilla extract, and chocolate to the bowl and stir to form a cake batter.

6. Pour the batter into your slow cooker.

7. Mix the caramelised condensed milk and double cream together in a bowl before adding to the slow cooker. Do not mix the milk into the batter. Instead, allow it to sit on top of the batter.

8. Add the lid and cook on high for 3 hours. You can test whether the batter is ready by inserting a knife into the middle of the cake. If it's ready, the knife will come out dry.

9. Serve up immediately so the cake is nice and warm. Add a scoop of ice cream, maple syrup, or chocolate sauce on top to make it extra delicious.

DESSERTS

SLOW COOKER CRÈME BRÛLÉE

Makes 6 servings
Preparation time – 5 minutes
Cooking time – 2 hours
Nutritional value per serving – 489 kcals,
27g carbs, 4g protein, 31g fat

INGREDIENTS

- ✔ 3 egg yolks
- ✔ 100ml whipping cream
- ✔ 100g sugar
- ✔ 1 tsp vanilla extract

METHOD

1. Combine the egg yolks, whipping, 50g of the sugar, and the vanilla extract in a bowl. Whisk to combine.

2. Place two rolls of tin foil into the bottom of your slow cooker and place 6 ramekins in between the two lines of tin foil to secure them in place.

3. Pour enough boiling water into the slow cooker to fill it to about one-third of the way up the ramekins.

4. Place the lid on the slow cooker and turn it on to a low heat. Cook for 2 hours until the custard topping is set.

5. Turn off the slow cooker and remove the ramekins. Leave them to set for around 6 hours.

6. Sprinkle with a bit of extra sugar and lightly torch using a culinary torch until the sugar on the top turns brown.

DESSERTS

PLAIN SLOW COOKER CHEESECAKE

Makes 8 servings
Preparation time – 15 minutes
Cooking time – 5 hours
Nutritional value per serving – 271 kcals,
21g carbs, 19g protein, 8g fat

INGREDIENTS

- ✔ 300g whole crackers
- ✔ 6 tbsp butter, melted
- ✔ 600g cream cheese
- ✔ 150g sour cream
- ✔ 100g sugar
- ✔ 5 eggs, beaten
- ✔ 3 tbsp plain flour
- ✔ 1 tsp vanilla extract

METHOD

1. Grease the inside of your slow cooker or line with parchment paper.

2. Place the crackers in a blender and pulse them into crumbs.

3. Add the melted butter into the blender and pulse to combine.

4. Pour the crumb mixture into the slow cooker and press down so that the top is smooth.

5. In a bowl, whisk together the cream cheese, sour cream, sugar, eggs, flour, and vanilla extract until fully combined.

6. Pour this mixture evenly over the crumb base in the slow cooker.

7. Place the lid on the machine and cook the cheesecake on a low heat for 6 hours.

8. Serve immediately or store in the fridge until you're ready to eat!

DESSERTS

SLOW COOKER VICTORIA SPONGE

Makes 8 servings
Preparation time – 10 minutes
Cooking time – 1-2 hours
Nutritional value per serving – 341 kcals,
28g carbs, 10g protein, 19g fat

INGREDIENTS

- ✔ 150g self-raising flour
- ✔ 150g unsalted butter
- ✔ 150g caster sugar
- ✔ 1 tsp baking powder
- ✔ 3 eggs, beaten

METHOD

1. Grease the inside of your slow cooker with a little butter or oil, or line it with some parchment paper.

2. Mix the flour, butter, caster sugar, and baking powder in a bowl until fully combined.

3. Pour in the beaten eggs and mix to combine.

4. Transfer this mixture into the slow cooker, add the lid, and cook on a high heat for 1-2 hours. The cake is cooked when you can insert a knife into the centre, and it comes out dry.

5. Remove from the slow cooker and leave to cool on a rack.

6. Slice into squares and serve up with some jam and whipped cream.

DESSERTS

SLOW COOKER SALTED CARAMEL BARS

Makes 8 servings
Preparation time – 10 minutes
Cooking time – 2 hours
Nutritional value per serving – 456 kcals,
45g carbs, 5g protein, 23g fat

INGREDIENTS

- ✔ 100g butter
- ✔ 200g sugar
- ✔ 1 tsp vanilla extract
- ✔ 1 egg, beaten
- ✔ 400g plain flour
- ✔ 100g caramel chocolate
- ✔ ½ tsp sea salt

METHOD

1. Grease your slow cooker with butter or oil or use parchment paper to line it.

2. Mix the butter, sugar, and vanilla extract together until light and fluffy.

3. Whisk in the eggs until fully combined.

4. Gradually add the flour, stirring constantly to mix. This should form a dough-like mixture.

5. Press half of the doughy mixture into the bottom of the slow cooker and even out the top.

6. Break up the caramel chocolate into small chunks and lightly press half of them into the base layer of dough.

7. Add the second half of the doughy mixture on top, followed by the remaining caramel chocolate chunks.

8. Sprinkle the sea salt evenly over the top before placing the lid on the slow cooker.

9. Turn on to a low heat and cook for 2-3 hours.

10. Once cooked, remove from the slow cooker, and leave to cool on a drying rack.

11. Cut into bars and serve. Store any leftovers in the fridge.

12. If you want to reheat the bars, pop them in the microwave for 30-60 seconds until warm.

SLOW COOKER STICKY GINGER CAKE

Makes 8 servings
Preparation time – 10 minutes
Cooking time – 4 hours
Nutritional value per serving – 325 kcals,
31g carbs, 15g protein, 24g fat

INGREDIENTS

- ✔ 200g unsalted butter, softened
- ✔ 150g caster sugar
- ✔ 50g muscovado sugar
- ✔ 4 eggs, beaten
- ✔ 200g self-raising flour
- ✔ 1 tsp ginger
- ✔ 1 tsp nutmeg
- ✔ 20g crystallised ginger, chopped into small pieces
- ✔ 1 tbsp golden syrup

METHOD

1. Grease the inside of your slow cooker with some butter or oil or line with parchment paper.

2. Mix the butter with both types of sugar until combined.

3. Fold in the eggs, followed by the flour, spices, crystallised ginger, and golden syrup. Stir until fully combined.

4. Pour the mixture into the slow cooker, place the lid on top, and turn onto a low heat.

5. Cook for 4 hours until the cake is cooked. This can be checked by inserting a knife into the centre of the cake. It should come out dry when the cake is ready.

6. Remove the cake from the slow cooker and leave to cool on a rack.

7. Serve with a drizzle of maple syrup and enjoy!

DESSERTS

SLOW COOKER VEGAN BLUEBERRY CAKE

Makes 4 servings
Preparation time – 15 minutes
Cooking time – 1-2 hours
Nutritional value per serving – 110 kcals,
15g carbs, 3g protein, 10g fat

INGREDIENTS

- ✔ 150g plain flour
- ✔ 1 tsp baking powder
- ✔ 1 tbsp ground flaxseed
- ✔ 2 tsp agave nectar or ½ tsp stevia

- ✔ 150ml vegan milk (any type)
  100g blueberries
- ✔ 1 tbsp applesauce or olive oil
- ✔ 1 tsp vanilla extract

METHOD

1. Grease the inner compartment of your slow cooker with some vegan butter oil or line with parchment paper.

2. Mix the flour, baking powder, and ground flaxseed in a bowl.

3. In another bowl, mix the agave nectar, milk, blueberries, applesauce or olive oil, and vanilla extract until combined.

4. Fold the dry mixture into the wet mixture before transferring into the slow cooker.

5. Pace the lid on the slow cooker and cook on high for 1-2 hours until the cake is cooked all the way through.

6. Serve immediately or leave to cool on a rack, ready to serve after dinner.

DESSERTS

SLOW COOKER VEGAN FUDGE

Makes 8 servings
Preparation time – 10 minutes
Cooking time – 2 hours
Nutritional value per serving – 346 kcals,
30g carbs, 10g protein, 22g fat

INGREDIENTS

- ✔ 100g plain flour
- ✔ 100g sugar
- ✔ 1 tbsp cocoa powder
- ✔ 1 tsp baking powder
- ✔ ½ tsp salt
- ✔ 200ml vegan milk (any type)
- ✔ 2 tbsp olive oil
- ✔ 1 tsp vanilla extract
- ✔ 200g vegan chocolate chips

METHOD

1. Line the slow cooker with parchment paper or grease with vegan butter or oil.

2. In a bowl, whisk together the flour, sugar, cocoa powder, baking powder, and salt until fully combined.

3. Pour in the milk, oil, and vanilla extract and stir to combine. Fold in half of the chocolate chips.

4. Pour the mixture into the slow cooker and spread into an even layer.

5. Sprinkle the remaining half of the chocolate chips evenly over the top of the batter.

6. Place the lid on the slow cooker and cook the batter for 2 hours on low.

7. Once cooked, remove the batter, and leave to cool on a rack before cutting into slices.

8. To serve, heat the fudge in the microwave for 30-60 seconds. Store any remaining fudge in the fridge.

DESSERTS

SLOW COOKER STICKY DATE PUDDING

Makes 6 servings
Preparation time – 30 minutes
Cooking time – 5 hours
Nutritional value per serving – 599 kcals,
67g carbs, 8g protein, 33g fat

INGREDIENTS

- ✔ 250g pitted dates, chopped
- ✔ 1 tsp baking soda
- ✔ 100g unsalted butter, softened
- ✔ 200g granulated sugar
- ✔ 1 tsp vanilla extract
- ✔ 2 eggs, beaten
- ✔ 350g self-raising flour
- ✔ 150g brown sugar
- ✔ 3 tbsp golden syrup

METHOD

1. In a bowl, mix the dates, baking soda, and 300ml boiling water.

2. In another bowl, combine the butter, granulated sugar, and vanilla extract until fluffy.

3. Fold in the beaten eggs, followed by the flour and dates (including the boiling water along with them).

4. Grease the slow cooker or line with parchment paper.

5. Pour in the sticky date batter into the slow cooker, followed by the brown sugar and golden syrup.

6. Pour 750ml boiling water into the slow cooker on top of the other ingredients to fully cover them.

7. Add the lid to the slow cooker and cook on a low heat for 4 hours.

8. Serve hot with some custard, ice cream, or maple syrup.

DESSERTS

SLOW COOKER APPLE AND RHUBARB CRUMBLE

Makes 8 servings
Preparation time – 10 minutes
Cooking time – 5 hours
Nutritional value per serving – 417 kcals,
64g carbs, 5g protein, 18g fat

INGREDIENTS

- ✔ 200g plain flour
- ✔ 150g unsalted butter, softened
- ✔ 100g brown sugar
- ✔ 100g rolled oats
- ✔ 1 tsp cinnamon
- ✔ 1 tsp nutmeg
- ✔ 600g apples, cut into chunks
- ✔ 400g rhubarb, cut into chunks
- ✔ 1 tbsp lemon juice

METHOD

1. Combine the flour, butter, brown sugar, oats, cinnamon, and nutmeg in a bowl until it resembles breadcrumbs.

2. Add the apples, rhubarb, and lemon juice to the slow cooker.

3. Spread the crumble mixture evenly over the top of the fruit.

4. Add the lid to the slow cooker and cook on a low heat for 5 hours until the rhubarb is cooked.

5. Serve up immediately with some custard or ice cream or leave to cool on a drying rack.

DESSERTS

DISCLAIMER

This book contains opinions and ideas of the author and is meant to teach the reader informative and helpful knowledge while due care should be taken by the user in the application of the information provided. The instructions and strategies are possibly not right for every reader and there is no guarantee that they work for everyone. Using this book and implementing the information/recipes therein contained is explicitly your own responsibility and risk. This work with all its contents, does not guarantee correctness, completion, quality or correctness of the provided information. Misinformation or misprints cannot be completely eliminated.

Printed in Great Britain
by Amazon

71312903R00066